THE SALES MANAGER'S
GUIDE TO SANITY

How to build a winning team, get better results, and keep most of your hair.

A Topic Based Guide for Sales Managers Everywhere

The Sales Manager's Guide to Sanity

Editing and Formatting Credits:
Mandie Jones
James Todd Lewis

Front Cover Credits:
Leslie Goupil Bax, Designamo, llc

Flourish and Breaks:
Leslie Goupil Bax, Designamo, llc

Revision 1.0.5

Contact e-mail: ecowdrey@salesmanagersguidetosanity.com

ISBN 978-1-940929-90-3 (print)

ISBN 978-0-578-04776-8 (eBook)

For

The best sales managers I have ever worked with:

Wynn Poole

Bill Chavent

Mitch Holmes

Renaud Rodrigue

Brian Balow

*And for my awesome wife Pamela who
continues to amaze me.*

*Special thanks to James Todd Lewis, Chris Kersey, and
Larry Hochman for the constructive feedback and
encouragement through this project.*

Table of Topics

Introduction

This is a guide for sales managers. It is written from the point of view of business to business sales, however, most, if not all of the principles discussed, can easily be applied to business to consumer sales teams as well.

This guide is designed to help both new and experienced sales managers deal with the unique and challenging role of managing a sales team.

Over the last 20 years, I have been fortunate enough to experience working within world class sales organizations including Xerox, Kodak, IKON, and Ricoh. While my personal experience is mostly within the copier/printer industry, I believe the principles of success and good sales management transcend all industries.

This guide is a collection of my experiences, advice from mentors, lessons from readings, and many other influences which have been important in shaping and developing my career.

I have had the great blessing of working for some wonderful people who have helped me along the way.

I have also worked with and for some idiots who had no business being a manager (they know who they are).

Lessons from both are equally important. It is my hope that you will able to take a few pointers from this guide to make your journey to becoming the best sales manager in your company run quickly, smoothly, and successfully!

This guide is not for sales representatives. Sales reps are supplied with plenty to read about how to be better sales people. Companies spend a lot of money training sales people on product, process, closing, style, and all the topics relating to sales.

There is not nearly enough investment made in creating great sales managers. I have found this to be true with both large and small companies.

The job of the sales manager is really, really hard. It is perhaps the most difficult job in the company for many reasons. First, you are expected to do what is best for the company while managing people who only want to do what is best for their wallet. Second, you are responsible for your team's results. You are no longer an individual contributor.

Remember, most sales managers were sales people first. There is an old saying that "the best sales people don't always make great managers."

I submit the only reason that is true is because no one taught them how to be a great manager. More often than not, a company will just promote the best sales person and tell them to create copies of themselves.

Guess what… That doesn't work! On other occasions, a company will promote a sales rep, send them to some one week managers training course and expect them to be great.

Guess what… That rarely works. Maybe you were not the best sales person, but you showed a talent for managing others. Maybe you lied in the interview. It really doesn't matter how you got here.

However you came to be a sales manager, you are here now and you need to create the NUMBER ONE team in the company.

Why? Because nothing else matters. When you have built a NUMBER ONE team, everything else will follow – money, recognition, promotion, and anything else you set your mind to.

It is my hope that this book will serve as a more of reference guide than a one-time read.

It is my hope this book will be something you can keep in your desk or on the shelf in your office so that you may come back to it in those moments when you need a little sanity, which in your role as sales manager, may be a little more often than you expected!

Your Real Job as a Sales Manager

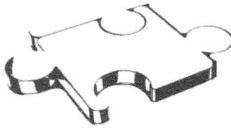

4 Concepts to Keep in Mind at All Times

Your real job, your <u>only</u> job, is to build the number one team in your company. Your job is to deliver results which <u>exceed</u> your manager's expectations. To do that, you need to focus on four things and four things only.

1. Build the best team you can. That means hiring the right members for your team.
2. Coach everyone to do better. That means being supportive, mentoring, and helping <u>every</u> member of your team.
3. Build a team culture that will excite and motivate your team.
4. Fire the ones who can't (or won't) do the job.

Read that again. It is really that simple.

Point number 1 is the most important. <u>Everything</u> starts with hiring the right people and building the best team you can possibly can.   There are no substitutes for great people.

Get great at recruiting and interviewing. When you have the right people, the results and the rewards are so much easier to attain.

The Mind of a Sales Rep

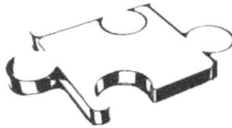

All sales people are in sales for <u>three reasons</u>. These three reasons are what motivate them every day. They are:

- Money
- Freedom
- Recognition

Everything else, and we mean ALL other goals, tie to these three motivators.

It is important that you do not assume you know the order of importance. Money is not always the most important. Each sales person is different and depending on their personal situation, these may have a different order of importance to each member of your team.

If these three motivators were not important, then your reps would be accountants, or teachers, or engineers, or some other job that kept them in a cube all day and had a fixed income.

It is your job to exploit the reasons people are on your team and use them as motivation.

Money

Sales people choose the sales profession because they want the potential of "unlimited" income.

- They want to make six figures.
- They want to be masters of their own success.
- They measure themselves and their self-worth by how much they make.

This is their primary score board of self-worth.

Your job is to help them work their compensation plan to its fullest potential. That <u>does not</u> mean work around the comp plan! That means work <u>to</u> the compensation plan.

When they see you are willing to help them get every nickel they have rightfully earned, they will go out and get more business.

If they see they are being "nickled and dimed" over loopholes in the comp plan, they will take steps to manipulate deals in their favor.

Freedom

Exploiting these motivations also means not doing things to block their goals.

For example, I have seen some senior sales managers take teams of highly experienced and tenured sales people and expect them to be at their desk at 8 AM every morning.

While the company's work hours may be 8 AM to 5 PM, experienced and proven sales people usually enjoy the freedom to run their own schedule. They should absolutely be allowed this freedom after they have EARNED THE RIGHT.

For sales people to earn the right to manage their own schedule, they need to keep to one simple principle:

"PERFORMANCE IS THE PRICE OF FREEDOM"

In sales, everyone is either "above the line" or "below the line." The rep is either over their quota or below their quota. There are no other measurements that really matter.

Let's be honest, if a rep is over their quota, what do you care where they are at 8 AM? If you feel the need to *control* your team, you should resign now. You will drive yourself crazy trying to *control* sales people.

If you can't trust an individual to self-motivate, self-start and work towards their goals, then get rid of them and find the ones who will.

Recognition

Recognition comes in many forms. Recognition can range from the company paid BIG trip at the end of the year to a simple name call out during a conference call.

Here is what you need to know as a manager. Recognition should be frequent, sincere, appropriate, and should come in different forms.

Most sales people do not fully understand how powerful recognition really is to their own happiness, self-drive, and self-worth. It is the one motivator they themselves have a hard time putting a value on if they are not satisfied. Often reps will come into your office and complain about working too many hours and not making enough money, but rarely will they complain about recognition (or lack of it) because it is so much less tangible than the other factors.

Make it tangible for them. If you don't believe how important recognition is to your team, then stop doing it and watch their morale disintegrate.

There you have it. It is really that simple. Figure out what is important to each member of your team and coach accordingly.

The Reasons You Win

The reasons you win are the reason you lose.

Ask any sales rep why they won a deal and they will respond with a variety of answers. They will say they won because of relationship, a great demo, outselling the competition, etc. They will never say they won because they offered the cheapest price. No one ever comes back to the office, rings the bell, and says "I won because I offered the lowest price."

However, ask a sales rep why they lost and nine times out of ten they will say ... you know it ... price. The truth is, no one ever wins or loses because of price. There are always, always other factors involved. Sure, price may be one of them, but it is never alone. Everyone who has been in sales for any period of time has had both of these calls from a customer at some point:

Call 1 – "Hey Ed, this is Jim, we are ready to buy, but I need you to be at price X. Get me that price and let's get the paperwork done."

Call 2 – This "call" is often an email, because customers don't want to tell you that you lost in person. The email usually looks like this…"Hey Ed, this is Jim, we decided to go with your competitor. Sorry Ed, you did a great job, we just felt it was best for the company and they were lower cost."

Why do you get Call 1? Because you have done a number of things right. Most likely, you have established a relationship better than your competition and demonstrated greater value. You have helped the customer to see a way to improve their business. You have earned the right to get this call and therefore understand the REAL price point at which the customer will buy.

Why do you get Call 2? Because the competition has done a better job, has a better relationship, and earned the right to get Call 1 instead of you. Notice in Call 2, the customer told me the competition was cheaper. Often that is either a lie, or an expression of the fact that he shared the buying price with someone other than you. No one buys on price alone.

Now that we know it is not price that wins…why do you win or lose? To win your reps must do the following four things:

1. Establish credibility and relationships with the right level of decision maker.

2. Understand your customers' business issues and requirements.

3. Present the right solution to meet the customers' requirements.

4. Convey your value proposition effectively. In other words, do a good job of selling and not a bad job of selling.

The challenge with this process is that it is difficult to measurable. As managers, you must focus on things you can measure (and therefore have an effect). We determined that the best exercise to measure how your reps are doing with any given deal is to establish ten tangible steps that help you win. This is very important because it will:

- increase your win rate, and
- improve your forecast accuracy.

Unfortunately, we cannot just give you a universal list of your ten tangible steps because these vary based on your company and your industry.

Below is a sample list to give you some ideas of what should be in the 10 steps. Note that anything that goes on this list must be *tangible, measurable,* and *easy to determine:*

10 Sample Steps (in no particular order)

1. Account research done prior to first call

2. Proposal presented to the decision maker

3. Customer has been qualified for credit and chosen method of payment

4. Demonstration has been attended by the decision maker

5. Customer's business issues have been identified, documented, and agreed to by the decision maker

6. Time frame to make a decision has been identified and agreed to by the customer

7. Customer has agreed that the proposed solution will solve their business issues. This may be done via a business case, return on investment exercise, or some other method to establish proof of concept.

8. Customer has contacted references

9. Strategic resources have been engaged such as service, a vendor resource, a technical analyst, etc.

10. Customer has attended an event or trade show with you.

Once you establish your 10 steps, you can then use them when discussing a deal with your reps. You can also start to make managerial judgments about your reps chances of really winning a deal.

For example:

- If a rep has completed less than 50% of the steps, your chances of winning are likely zero.
- If a rep has completed 50% to 70% of the steps, you likely have a 50/50 chance of winning.
- If a rep has completed 80% of the steps or greater, you likely have an 80%+ chance of winning.

These results will vary slightly, but they are a solid indicator that will give you the ability to help your reps win more and improve your forecast accuracy (good management!).

6 Keys to Hosting Great Team Building Events

Why hold team building events? Results!

Having a "team" means they should act as a team and not a group of individuals. To get a group of type A, high-flying, high-strung, self-absorbed sales people (exactly who I want on my team), you <u>must</u> do team building events off site.

The end goal is to have a team who go to each other for answers and help, instead of coming straight to you all the time.

Team building helps in a number of ways.

First, people get to know other on a more personal level. They drop their guard and start to talk to each other as people.

Second, it improves morale. The team starts to feel like you and the company actually cares about them as people (and not just the results they produce).

Third, personality issues and conflicts get resolved or at least minimized. It is hard to hold a grudge against someone you played golf with and had a beer with afterwards.

Lastly, it improves communication and trust. Trust being the most important.

Here are six guidelines for great team events:

Do it on a regular basis. Regardless of whether your team is spread out all over the country, the region, or all in the same office, you must make it happen. Take them offsite and do a team building activity at least once per quarter. You will, of course, get budget objections from your manager, depending on your company. Get creative, build a business case, yell and scream, do whatever it takes to make this happen.

It really makes a difference. For example, while working for a former employer, we used to hold team building events on a regular basis. Morale was high and results were higher. When we were bought out by another company, all the team building stopped, morale dropped, as did results.

Mix up the types of activities. Don't just take everyone to play golf every time.

Here are some examples to help get you started. Some people suggest that the activities should not be competitive. I don't agree with that entirely. Golf, Laser Tag, Putt Putt, beach games and yard games like egg toss or corn hole are great.

Include some training in the day. No more than a quarter to a half day. Have a vendor come in and present. Frequently a vendor will give you money to fund the event so that can be an added bonus if you play your cards right. Everyone likes training and your boss will most likely buy in if you have this as part of the day.

Include some recognition in the day. Remember, sales people are sales people for three reasons (see "The Mind of the Sales Rep"). Give out little awards for anything and everything. A great customer letter, targets reached or exceeded etc.

Let your team do the planning. You don't want them to plan all the events, but let them plan some of them. Planning in itself is a team building activity. They will be more excited and more satisfied when the day comes.

Make it for and about your team only. Don't invite your boss or other managers. Your team may not relax with other managers around and you will defeat the purpose of the day.

5 Best Practices of Managing Up

Managing up – This is often a *critical* function of your role as a sales manager. Too many times it is underdone or completely overdone.

You need to let your boss know that your team is doing a great job on a regular basis. Notice the emphasis on "your TEAM" doing a great job, not "YOU" doing a great job. If you recognize and advertise your peoples' success then you will be associated with it. Never promote your own success. Always promote the success of your team or team members.

Adopt the attitude that your team is YOUR team and the members of YOUR team are more important than yourself. If someone asks why you are having a great year, the answer is "Thanks, I have a really great team."

So how do you effectively manage up? Here are five pointers that will help you manage up more effectively.

1. Send out regular communications about deals your team members have closed. Describe how hard-fought the battle was, who your competitors were, why your rep won, and how much money the company made as result. Send it to your team and copy in all your management structure.

2. Send a private email to your boss describing how greatly improved one or more of your reps is. Even if they are behind plan, you can send a note saying "Hey boss, just wanted you to know that Stephen has grown his sales 25% year over year from this same quarter last year. He is still behind plan, but his funnel indicates he will finish over plan for the year."

3. Recognize other cross-functional organizations in email or on conference calls. Tell everyone how the service tech or technical analyst was instrumental in closing the deal. Stress the team effort approach.

4. The frequency with which you do this is important and really depends on your organizational culture. Usually, once a month is plenty. Try not to do this more than once per month. People should look forward to your recognition and not ignore it because it seems contrived.

5. Fight for your people. Go to bat for them. Most upper level managers recognize this as a positive trait. When you do go to bat, be prepared to discuss why your request is good for your rep

AND good for the company. If you can blend in how it is good for the customer, then you have the trifecta!

Building Your Team

A Sales Managers Approach to Finding the Best People

"*You don't build a business. You build people and then people build the business.*"
- Zig Ziglar

Truer words have never been spoken when it comes to team building. Building a business means building a team. You know that the single most important task you have is to find and hire the best people. The truth is that actually finding the best people is much harder than it sounds.

The process of recruiting, interviewing, and hiring can be lengthy, time consuming, frustrating, and even boring at times, but it leads to what you want the most…the best team.

So how do you find the best people? The key is start with a sound hiring process. Depending on the size and resources of your company, there may already be a process in place. If not, it may be up to you to develop, improve, and implement a hiring process. Before we get to the hiring process, you need to find great candidates. Here are some best practices for finding candidates in the new economy.

> **Stop Trolling** – In other words, stop posting jobs and waiting for candidates to send you a resume. This of course requires you make a big change in your mind set. The old tradition of posting of job and waiting for the candidates too come to you is easy and tempting to rely upon, but it probably will not get you the best sales people. Recently, we posted a sales job opening in Washington, DC. We got 121 resumes. You probably don't have time to sort through 121 resumes and expect any real quality results. We did and here is what we found. 90 of the 121 candidates were currently unemployed. Let's face it, how many really good unemployed sales people do you know? Sure, everyone has a story and some of them are actually true. There are some really great people out there who have lost their jobs, but sadly, it is very difficult for you as a hiring manager to sort through the stories.

> **Become the hunter** – You must be the one seeking candidates instead of the candidates seeking you. There are simply too many people looking for jobs. You must become surgical in your approach. You must be the one seeking candidates instead of the candidates seeking you. You must go out and find that award winning rep that is employed, successful, not necessarily looking for job, but may be just unhappy enough to talk to you.

Use a recruiter – This can be expensive, but using recruiters that are specialists in your industry can be well worth the money.

Use on-line search tools – Most of job sites out there like The Ladders, Monster, etc., have search tools that allow you to search for candidates based on criteria you select. LinkedIn has also developed into one of the best recruiting platforms out there. You have to sign up for the Premium service, but it allows you to specifically search for people who may not actually be looking at the time. There are several "how to" guides out there to give you specifics about how to use LinkedIn. One we like is referenced in the Resources section of this book at the end (Jorgen Sunberg). Do some homework and you will find several others out there.

Ask your customers – One of the best candidates I ever hired came from asking several customers one question. *"Other than my rep, who is your favorite sales person that calls on you regularly and why?"*

Ask your team – Great sales people tend to know other great sales people. They know who their competitors are and who is effective.

Once you have identified a strong list of potential candidates, it is time to take them through the process. Having a check list is particularly important in the hiring process because it helps you to maintain some objectivity. Every sales manager in history has at some point made a poor hiring choice. Most have made several poor choices.

It is one of the hazards of the job. Many will tell you that the poor choices happened for a variety of reasons including not following a process, rushing through process, skipping steps, and becoming "sold" on a candidate that we really like. Following a check list makes mistakes less likely to happen.

Below is a sample hiring process that has been used may many successful sales managers:

1. **Write a highly detailed job description** – List everything you are looking for in a new member of your team. You may need to get help with this from HR or even an outside firm. This is the critical first step. If you don't have a great job description, you don't know who you are really looking to hire.

2. **Resume Review** – Read the entire resume. Jot down questions in the margin. Look up the candidate on Facebook, LinkedIn, and other social media sites. Do the stories match up?

3. **Phone Interview** – Keep these short and have a planned structure for the call. Are you selling them or are they selling you? The only purpose of the phone interview is to determine if you want a face to face interview.

4. **In Person Interview with yourself** – You must interview all your candidates in person. No video calls. You need to get a "feel" for the whole person you are thinking about bringing onto your team. This just doesn't work well on video calls. I have done dozens of them and it is just not the

same. For example, the candidate may be flustered with the technology and not "show" well. You may have technology issues like slow internet connections that hamper the interview. A thousand things can prevent you from having a quality interview. It can cut both ways. If you are trying to steal someone from the competition, you want to be face to face.

5. **In Person Interview with another manager** – None of us are perfect and other managers are less emotionally attached to your pursuit of building your team. Have another manager take the candidate through a face to face interview. It is almost a guarantee that they will discover things you did not.

6. **In Person Interview with a member of your team** – Part of team building is finding people who share that X factor, that "chemistry", with other members of your team. Have one of your better do a ride along day, or just go to lunch with the candidate. The candidate will likely open up or ask revealing questions to another rep vs. talking with you as the manager. This also gains buy-in from your team which is an important extra benefit.

7. **Personality Test** – I was once a non-believer, but after having taken several tests myself and then used testing in the interview, I am a convert. These tests absolutely have a place in the hiring process. They can reveal much about a candidate. There are many services out there that can do this for your company. Find one and try it out. One

caution, use the test results as an added opinion, and not as a pass/fail gate in the interview process.

8. Final Interview and Offer – Take all the information from all the sources listed above and conduct one final interview. See if it all fits. See if there are holes in their story. Then, make the decision to extend an offer.

Interviewing is a real art. It takes time and lots of practice to get really good at it. Preparation is key to an interview going well.

Candidates are more educated and more practiced at answering interview question then ever before. Many companies have adopted a style of interviewing called "behavioral interviewing." There are classes, courses, and book after book about interviewing. You must get good at interviewing. Below is a brief on behavioral interviewing and some sample interview questions.

Behavioral interviewing is about asking candidates questions that reveal how they have acted in the past in certain situation. This is about discovering their actual thought process. It is not about getting a good answer. It drives at uncovering someone's real experience vs. a planned response.

The foundation of this approach requires you to first determine what key behaviors you are looking for in a sales rep. You can imagine that these behaviors are quite different from behavior you want in a service technician. For example, some behaviors managers find important in a sales rep include whether or not the candidate is goal oriented, can overcome adversity, is achievement driven, is good at presentations and communication, and is ethical. You need to determine these for yourself based on your company, industry, etc..

Below are some sample questions. For each question you want to take your time. You may only get through 2 to 4 questions during a 1 hour interview. Here is the methodology for each question:

1. Ask the question and give them time to digest and think of a good scenario.
2. Ask what was the situation and outcome.
3. What did he/she do (key points along the way)?
4. What did he/she say (key interactions along the way)?

The idea is do a deep dive into each question. Ask the candidate to "put you in the room" and describe who was there, what was the room like, what happened, and how others present reacted. This will help quickly see if the candidate is telling you a story or telling you the truth. It will also help you see if they describe the behavior you are looking to uncover.

Sample Sales Interview Scorecard

Name of Candidate:	
Date of Interview:	
Marketplace for Consideration:	

<u>Interview Questions</u>

Score Key: 0 = did not answer to satisfaction

1 = Partial Credit   2 = Full Credit

(Indicate score in the margin to the left of the question)

1. **GOAL ORIENTED:** *Give me an example of an important goal which you had set in the past and tell me about your success in reaching it.*

2. **GOAL ORIENTED:** *How do you achieve your monthly sales target?*

3. **Achievements and Accomplishments:** *From your past, talk about an important deal that you WON. What was the sales cycle like? What were the key challenges? What were the factors that lead to your success?*

4. **Achievements and Accomplishments:** *From your past, talk about an important deal that you LOST. What was the sales cycle like? What were the key challenges? What were the factors that lead to the deal doing to someone else?*

5. **Presentation, Persuasion and Verbal Skills:** *Tell me about a time when you obtained a new customer through networking activities.*

6. **Presentation, Persuasion and Verbal Skills:** Describe the most significant or creative presentation that you have had to complete.

7. **Presentation, Persuasion and Verbal Skills:** *Give me an example of a time when you obtained a customer through cold calling and prospecting. How did you approach the customer?*

8. **Integrity and Ethics:** *Give me an example of a time when your integrity was tested and yet prevailed in a selling situation.*

9. **Overcoming Adversity:** *During a presentation, what would you do if you realize that you have gathered some wrong information? How would you rectify your mistake?*

10. **Overcoming Adversity:** *Tell me about an instance where you had to handle a group of unsatisfied customers.*

6 Requirements for Presenting a Business Case

The margin on zero... is zero.

As a sales manager, you are often faced with decisions regarding negotiating a deal. Sometimes those parameters are well-defined by your company and sometimes they are not. Most of the time, sales managers have a set of guidelines under which they may approve deals.

When one of your team members brings you a deal with some customer demand, how do you help your rep negotiate? How do you analyze the demands of the customers and weigh it against the needs of the company? How do you go to your manager and fight to get the deal?

As a sales manager, you need to be prepared to present the business case for your company to approve taking the deal. Depending on your company's corporate culture, that business case may need to be stronger on certain key performance measurements. Those may include pricing, terms and conditions, and many other factors. Here are some key elements to presenting a strong business case:

1. **Background on the customer:** Is this a net new customer that you are stealing from a competitor? Is this a long time loyal customer?

2. **Benefit to the Customer:** Why is important to the customer that they choose your solution? Don't overlook this important element. This may seem "obvious," but it may reveal something important to your company's strategy.

3. **Benefit to the Company:** Is the customer in a position to become a reference or are they one already? Is the customer's business strong and growing? Can winning this deal lead to others this year?

4. **Benefit to your Rep or Team:** This is a chance to "manage up" a little and discuss what a great year your rep is having, or how this will get them to President's Club, or how this will be the first placement in a much desired vertical market that everyone has been chasing.

5. **Revenue:** What will this deal mean in terms of total revenue to your company? That means the total stream of equipment, service, consumables, and all other revenue streams that will stem from this deal over the entire term of the agreement.

6. **Margin:** At the end of the day, this is the most important element, but it needs to come last (especially if the deal is somewhat skinny). This is why you have gone to the trouble to write up all

these other win-win elements. You probably need an exception that you cannot approve and now you have arrived at this point. State what the company will make now and over the term. Then remind your manager, or whoever you are presenting to, that THE MARGIN ON ZERO IS ZERO, and that if you allow your competitor to take the deal, the company will lose all of the above AND the available margin on the table. Does your company want the margin, or do they want to give it to the competition?

4 Pillars of Great Expectation Setting

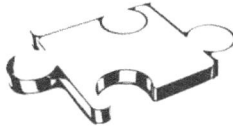

Perhaps the most important single action you can take as the leader of your team is to ensure you set proper expectations which are firm, clear, measurable, and well thought out. Setting expectations is often taken for granted in larger companies because there are so many company policies, handbooks, and other resources. Remember, this is YOUR team, and YOU need to set clear directions and expectations in order to achieve goals.

Here are some key elements for setting good expectations:

First, expectation setting should be done in public (at least in the public arena of your team). The best time to do so is at a face to face team meeting. You may also want to post these in your office.

Second, expectation setting should be done in writing. Below is a sample expectations document. You should write your own, put it on company letter head, and hand a copy to everybody on the team. And yes, have them sign it after you review it.

Third, the expectation should have buy-in or agreement from the team. Cover your written document. Explain to them each element and why it is good for the team and good for them as individuals. Ask for questions, concerns, additions. *Deletions are not allowed* because these are your minimum standards.

Lastly, you need to stress to your team that these are the MINIMUM ACCEPTABLE STANDARDS. They are the Team's standards and not just yours. These are not *nice to have*. These are *requirements for membership of your team*. You do not have to be rude, loud or domineering about this, but you absolutely must be firm and clear.

The ideal timing is at the beginning of a new year, but you can really do it at any time. Once you set the expectations, be prepared to stick to them. You must be prepared to make an example of anyone breaking the rules.

This does not necessarily mean firing them, but it does mean, at a minimum, calling them out. If you do not call out the offenders, neither you nor your expectations will be respected or realized.

For example, We once had a rep who was always late for team meetings. We did two things to call him out and make the point. The first time, we locked the door so he had to knock to get in. We made him wait and knock several times before we let him in. The second time it happened, we moved to a different conference room. That ended it. He was never late again. Another manager told me that he would have rule breakers present in front of the team as a means of "punishment." It would be "on the spot" and usually something hard, such as a new application, product, or process. The embarrassment was usually enough to end it.

Sample:

SALES TEAM MEMBER EXPECTATIONS Document

1. Time Management
   i. Be on all calls (On Time)
   ii. Be at all training (On Time)
   iii. Put in a full day and a full week (8 to 5 is the minimum)
2. Reporting and Accountability
   i. Be responsive to requests from management
   ii. Keep Outlook Calendar up to date
   iii. Keep your CRM up to date
   iv. Keep the team and management informed of all relevant actions (time off, customer issues, etc)
   v. Maintain the confidentiality of company information
3. Be Accessible and Responsive
   i. Return all calls and emails quickly (To co-workers, management, and customers)
4. Be Respectful to Other Team Member(s)
   i. Praise in public, deal with conflict in private
   ii. Maintain a positive attitude in the bullpen
   iii. Offer to help your team mates whenever possible
5. Generate Results
   i. Consistent, reliable performance
   ii. Deals are clean and adhere to ethical standards
6. Strive to make this a GREAT place to work
   i. A positive, professional, ethical, success driven environment

Employee Name _____

Employee Signature _____

Date_____

Building a World-Class Sales Team Culture

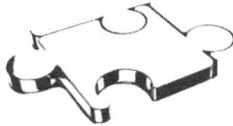

As a sales manager, you must set the expectations for your team. Team expectation setting is normally a one time, or at least once a year, event. Building a team culture is an ongoing activity. The best sales managers work very hard at this on a daily or weekly basis. They build a culture of teamwork, high performance, and success. Your team culture can influence the team every day and at every event, in either a positive or negative manner.

The culture of your team and your company is perhaps the single most influential factor on results. Think about this as if you are a sales rep. You come to work and the tone in the office is one of distrust, rumors, favoritism, lies, self protection, poor service, and deceit. How do you feel and how motivated are you?

Compare that to coming to work in an environment of trust, integrity, transparency, communication, and encouragement. Now, how do you feel and how motivated are you?

Here are the DO's and DON'Ts of building a world-class team culture:

DO ADOPT A THEME FOR THE YEAR – A team needs a theme! That is why sports teams have names. A team should have some identity that they can take pride in. This produces healthy competition and comradely. Maybe it is as simple as geography. For example, you may have a Denver Team and a Richmond Team. You may adopt something more spirited. Such as, you may have a Sales Tigers and a Sales Stars team. Letting your team have some input is a great idea. It gives them buy-in, ownership, and pride. One caution is you may need to monitor the naming. You do not want the team to name itself anything that may be HR sensitive!

Once you have a name, then you need a theme. There are lots of great theme ideas out there. I am a big fan of the author Mac Anderson. He has written dozens of great business books. He publishes many of his works through http://www.simpletruths.com (by the way, I didn't get paid to advertise this). This is a great reference resource. There are many others, but this one is a great place to start.

For example, the theme we used last year was 212° (by Mac Anderson). There is a book, a plaque, a poster, and other little items you can buy that are all designed with that theme. The idea is that 212° is the boiling point of water. At 211 nothing happens, but one extra degree of effort makes all the difference. We even had team shirts made with the company logo on the chest, the team name on the right hand sleeve, and 212° on the other sleeve. The book came with a movie on a CD. We gave a copy of the book to every member of the team after we wrote a personal inscription. We played the movie at team meetings to get everyone excited. It works great! You can even set "stretch" goals for team members to earn their shirt. Talk about an easy performance enhancer!

This is just one example of a theme. There are many great ideas out there. Pick one that is appropriate for your team and have fun with it. The important part is having a theme to run with.

DO CLEAR THE DECKS – Process for the sake of process spells death to the high performing sales team. Keep you sales management process to a minimum. Feeling the need to track anything more than a rep's calendar and their pipeline (via CRM if you have one) is overkill. If you do not help them maximize time in front of customers, how can you expect them to hit their goals and deliver results?

DO COACH – Coaching and counseling are perhaps the most rewarding parts of being a sales manager. Helping and supporting your people to achieve their goals, helping them to be smarter, helping them to be better at what they do, is the ultimate in job satisfaction. It will also produce the ultimate results. There is a big difference in a team that runs to a coach for help and one that runs to a manager for help.

DO RECOGNITION – This is one of the BIG THREE as far as your team are concerned. Recognition for the individual and the team as a whole should be frequent, sincere, appropriate, and should come in different forms. This means everything from the Presidents Club trip to a simple shout out on your weekly call. NEVER do any meeting or conference call without some sort of recognition.

DO FIGHT FOR YOUR PEOPLE – Especially in big companies, it is easy to get lost in policy, politics, and the proverbial "sales prevention society" which seems to live in all organizations. Your role is help remove obstacles so your people can get deals done and pushed through "the system."

DO INVOLVE YOUR TEAM – Many sales managers, especially new sales managers, try to make all the decisions, do all the work, do all the planning, and close all the deals. That is a definite recipe for disaster. Involve your team in planning and running team meetings. Involve your team in presenting at team meetings. Involve your team in planning customer events. They are the ones who will benefit so why should they not help? One positive side effect of involvement is the ever-necessary element of buy-in and self-ownership. Without these, the team will always be marginal.

DO WORK HARD AND PLAY HARD – Expect and demand, yes DEMAND, hard work. It is important that your team sees you not just as a coach, but a human coach. Lead by example and get to work early, stay late, and do all the things you expect them to do.

You also need to take time off and disconnect. Read that again…disconnect. No emails, conference calls, or phone calls. The business will still be there when you get back. Leave one of your team as the "acting manager" and take a Friday off or take a vacation. They need to see that time off is acceptable as long as everyone is accountable for their time.

Too many managers make the mistake of thinking they cannot go for a beer with their team after work. This is perfectly fine and it's actually a mistake to not do. Just don't cross the line by getting drunk or staying too late, or behaving in a way that does not set a good leadership example.

DO BEST PRACTICE SHARING – Want to have your team raving about the next team meeting? Have each team member share a best practice. This could be an ROI example that got a deal closed or a demonstration skill. It could be an internal process that they mastered. Let's face it, great sales people figure out how to get things done. Have them share the knowledge with the rest of the team. It may be the most valuable exercise you can have them do.

DO ENCOURAGE SELF-DEVELOPMENT – There is an old saying… "leaders are readers." Find a good sales book that you like and buy everyone a copy. Make a book club out of it and discuss the book at the next team meeting and also help your team to identify and improve upon weaknesses. I had a team member that was a great rep, but was completely unskilled at Microsoft Excel. How anyone can get by in this day and age without having good Excel skills is beyond me, but it happens. I had that team member take an online class. Guess what, they had their eyes opened and were extremely appreciative. It also saved me a lot of personal time because I didn't have to stop and help them with the basics.

DON'T PLAY FAVORITES – Favoritism is the kiss of death to a sales manager. One, everyone will see it. Two, everyone, including the favorites, will lose respect for you. Three, people will leave the team. Four, it can get you into real trouble with your HR department and last but not least, it is just plain wrong.

DON'T LET ANYONE BE NEGATIVE ABOUT YOUR TEAM MEMBERS – This is a little like taking care of your team as if they are family. No one but you can yell at or discipline your children. Adopt the same mind-set. No one but you can criticize your team members. Defend them. They will hear about it and they will respect you. Fail to defend them and the reverse is true.

DON'T MAKE ANY DECISIONS THAT YOU ARE NOT WILLING TO POST ON YOUR OFFICE DOOR – There are no secrets. Accept that now. No matter how many policies your company has about salary, quota, etc.   People will talk.   If you make decision about something, be prepared for everyone to find out.

DON'T MICRO-MANAGE – Manage to your set expectations. Don't get tied up with the little stuff. Sales people loath micro-managers. Do not be one. They will not respect you or perform for you. Remember, you can't teach greed. If you feel like you have to micro-manage your team, then you have the wrong team (or team member).

Building a world-class team culture takes real work and it takes time. However, it is the difference between a good team and a great team. It is the path to long-term success as a sales manager.

9 Tips to Managing a Multi-Generational Sales Team

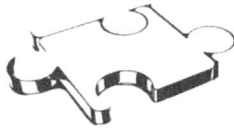

It is no longer uncommon for a sales manager to be managing a team people who are widely diverse in age. In fact, it is now possible that the sales team may have three or even four generations on the team at the same time. The sales manager may have members on the team – some of whom are younger, some of whom are older than the manager. Here are some definitions to consider:

Generation Ys, also known as "millennials", are considered to have been born in 1978 or later. Now, there are more than 70+ million of them and growing. They generally love technology, working as a team (family centric), and crave attention which means they love immediate feedback from many sources.

Generation Xs, or Gen Xers, are considered to have been born between 1965 and 1977. They make up about 44 to 50 million of the population. They are independent, free thinking, individualistic, and tend to focus to work/family balance.

Baby Boomers, born between 1946 and 1964, make up 80+ million in number. They are highly competitive and think workers should pay their dues. They are independent, free thinking, and work-centric.

Traditionalists, born 1945 and earlier, prefer clear expectations and direction, a logical approach to business, fair and consistent treatment, and formal respect with all communications. Traditionalists do not respond well to managers who are indecisive, disorganized, too tactile or "touchy-feely," use profanity, and worry about unpopular decisions.

Here are 9 tips to managing a multi-generational team:

1. Set clear expectations. Different generations may perceive standards differently. Be clear, concise, and get the teams buy-in.

2. Give plenty of recognition and feedback. Ask the team for recommendations about recognition and embrace a variety of types.

3. Use different formats for meeting and trainings. Use the web, conference calls, and in person meetings. Mix it up so that the various generations get a turn at their preferred method.

4. Get a clear understanding of every team members goals. The goals of Gen Y are likely to be focused on recognition and team work, whereas the goals of the Baby Boomer may be focused on freedom. Have them write down their goals and timelines for achieving them. You will be surprised what you learn!

5. Establish Mentor/Mentee relationships between team members from different generations. Have the Gen Ys teach the Baby Boomers about social media and have the Baby Boomers share their problem solving experience with the Gen Ys.

6. Create trust and cooperation on the team by organizing off site team events. This will help to break down barriers and improve communications. You may have to conduct specific exercises to make the different generation's team up.

7. Guard against perceptions, stereotypes, and mistrust. This boils down to communication. You may have to bring two employees into a room to discuss their differences. This can be difficult, but it is necessary, and almost always helps to clear the air.

8. Always relate conflict back to the team's goals and expectations. Do not allow anyone to deviate from the plan and always be consistent in decision-making.

9. Do your homework! Study up on the traits of the different generations. There's a lot of information out there. Seek it out and apply what fits for your team.

10 Rules for Terminating Sales People

As a sales manager, the most important thing you can do is hire great people. Your success literally begins and ends with the quality of the people you place on your team. Unfortunately, no matter how careful you are, no matter how much process you put a candidate through, sometimes you get the wrong one. Terminating an employee is an arduous task. It has real implications for the team, the company, and obviously for the employee and their family. Firing must be done the right way to prevent lawsuits and damage to team morale. There are several keys to the termination process, but before we get to those, a true story:

Recently, we hired a new sales rep. Let's call him "Jerry." Jerry was hired for one of our satellite offices, and after we put him through the proverbial "wringer" during the hiring process, we were excited to bring him on board and fly him to our HQ location in Denver. As with many companies, the first week of on-boarding is critical to an employee's success. We call it Boot Camp.

Jerry was all set, on a Monday morning, to leave his home on the East Coast, catch an early flight to connecting flight, and be picked up in Denver at 10:40 AM Mountain Time. Here is where the story really begins.

Jerry called me around 8 am on Monday morning to inform me that he had been in a car accident and had missed the first flight and therefore would miss the connection. He was working diligently with the airline and would get back to me with an arrival time. I thought to myself, "Okay, life happens, we can get caught up after missing a half day...no worries." Jerry finally arrived in Denver sometime around 10 PM on Monday night. I picked him up on Tuesday morning and we were at the office at 7:45 AM on Tuesday morning for an 8 AM start.

On Tuesday afternoon, after barely only a half day of training completed, Jerry started to complain of not feeling well. In fact, he stated he was feeling so ill in the stomach that needed to go back to the hotel and lie down.

Okay, now I'm worried, but still giving Jerry the benefit of the doubt. I thought it was maybe related to the car accident.

So, Wednesday comes, I don't hear from Jerry at all. In fact, he turned his phone off. The only contact I had with him was when I called the hotel and had them ring his room.

Thursday morning and I go down to breakfast early at 6 AM, and there is Jerry. He is standing there in his pajamas (really!) waiting to get some breakfast. He doesn't look sick, in fact, the look on his face was more of shock to see me so early. I asked him how he was feeling and he repeated how ill he was and how he couldn't keep any food down. Keep in mind, he was standing there holding a banana and a box of cereal.

I asked if I could take him to the doctor and he said he was still so weak that all he wanted to do was just lie down. He said he would try to "rally" and contact me by mid-morning. 10 AM came and went. All day I tried calling, texting, and emailing. I didn't hear from him again until I returned to the hotel at 6:30 PM. I called him from the front desk and asked him to come and talk. He declined, stating that he was still so sick. Here comes the good part...I reminded him that I was his ride to the airport and I was leaving the hotel at 7:45 AM, not 7:46 AM.

Friday morning, Jerry shows up on time, looking fine, but still complaining about being sick. After 15 minutes of silence in the car, here is how the conversation went...

Ed: "Jerry, do you want this job?"

Jerry: "Oh yes, very much, I am sorry I missed training, but I am sure I can catch up. Can you come spend next week with me?"

Ed: *(to myself) "We just spent thousands of dollars on you, and you are asking me to drop everything I had planned for next week and come give you another week after the week you just wasted?"*

Ed: "Jerry, may I ask why you didn't go to the doctor this week?"

Jerry: "I was too sick to go to the doctor."

Ed: *(to myself)* *"Did he really just say that?"*

The rest of the car ride was Jerry "talking the talk" and trying to re-sell me on his talents and all his contacts. Needless to say, I wasn't buying it. I left him at the check-in counter at the airport with this message...

"Jerry, this has been a very disappointing week. You are really so far behind that it will be difficult to catch you up. I would like to call you over the weekend after I have had a chance to think about how to plan this out."

He agreed and we went our separate ways. My real purpose for the delay was to give myself time to think, confer with HR, and do one more review with other managers before I let him go. I wanted to be sure I was doing the right thing.

Jerry didn't answer his phone all weekend (just like the whole prior week). On Monday morning, I called my HR Director and informed him of what had happened, and then I sent Jerry an email releasing him from employment on the grounds of "Failing to complete training and other basic requirements of a new employee as stated in the company handbook." He wouldn't answer the phone, but he answered the email with a myriad of anger, including accusations of unfair treatment, criticism of myself and the company, and pleading for his job back with promises of immediate revenue. His response more than confirmed that we made the correct decision.

There is much to be learned from this story, but the real point is that sales managers are often faced with less than clear-cut situations of poor employee conduct, which are not always 100% performance based. When and how do you decide to keep an employee or fire them? In the case above, we decided that it boiled down to a simple measurement: had Jerry acted reasonably? We clearly had legal grounds to fire him (failure to complete training), but was it the "right thing" to do?

Did Jerry act reasonably? Jerry could have:

1. Gone to the doctor and gotten a note as a measure of good faith.
2. Shown up and thrown up! At which point I would have taken him to the doctor.
3. He could have, at a minimum, communicated with me (his manager).

Unfortunately, he did none of the above and therefore did not act reasonably. I went to each manager in the company and we all agreed that if Jerry could act so unreasonably in this situation, there would probably be more issues with his unreasonable behavior in the future and we should let him go. Sometimes, you have to trust yourself, cover your bases, and make the call. In this case, we were put in a very difficult position and could not follow all the rules as described below. As a sales manager, you may not always be able to get it perfect, but you can get it right.

The moral is this…once you have a problem with an employee, you can either try to help them improve their performance, or fire them. Those are your only real options.

Here are some rules to the process the next time you have to make the call:

Rule 1 – Work with your HR department and always keep them informed. They can be of great help to you and can share the process you need to follow.

Rule 2 – Follow your company policy to the letter. If it is a performance related issue, you may need to deliver one or several written warnings first. It is often not a shock to the employee when the day comes. Many employees will actually fire themselves after one or two warning letters!

Rule 3 – Trust your gut instinct. People make mistakes and have problems. Are they worth keeping and did they act reasonably when confronted?

Rule 4 – Document everything leading up to the termination. Document every conversation, email, phone call, etc.

Rule 5 – "No breath is actually better than bad breath." Once you decide that an employee will not make it, start the process and get them out. Keeping a bad apple can literally spoil the barrel and do serious damage to your team's morale. Your team will respect you for it.

Rule 6 – Be respectful and professional when you give the employee the news. Terminate in person whenever possible. Be direct. A great manager of mine once told me, "There is no good way to do it," just tell them, "We are letting you go; this is the exit process we need to follow."

Rule 7 – Do not engage in discussions about performance or argue in any way. Simply tell them "The time for those discussions has passed. The decision is made and we now need to follow the exit process."

Rule 8 – Never make the decision alone. Always involve your HR department and your manager.

Rule 9 – Always fire in private, such as an office or conference room. Never be alone in the room when you give the news. Always have another manager with you and an HR rep if possible.

Rule 10 – Have a plan. Be prepared to brief your team, with no details, that the employee is no longer with the company and how the team will function until that employee is replaced. Be sure you never discuss the specifics of why someone is no longer with the company with anyone other than a manager.

3 Rules to Keep You Out of Sales Manager Land

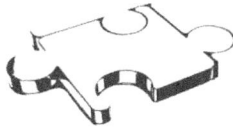

Sales managers are often faced with a multitude of tasks. You are expected to forecast, deal with customer issues, attend conference calls, interview candidates, fill out endless spreadsheets, deal with HR issues, and the lists goes on and on before you ever get to help your team sell anything. It is easy to get lost in "sales manager land." A long time ago, one of my favorite managers shared some lessons in prioritizing what you do every day with me. I now call these "the three rules of touch."

Touch Rule #1: "<u>Touch" every team member every</u> <u>day</u>. Sales reps by nature are needy. It is important that you 'touch' every member of your team every day. It might be a walk around the office while stopping to chat at each cube. It may be a phone call. The "touch" does not have to be about business per se. It can be about anything so long as you have contact with them. This inspires communication, reinforces the concept that you care about and support them, and helps to create an environment that allows them to motivate themselves.

Touch Rule #2: <u>Install the "touch it twice" rule</u>. The "touch it twice" rule is simple. Before a rep is allowed to bring you a problem, question, or issue, they must attempt to resolve, solve, or answer the question at least two times on their own. This helps you stem the endless flow of issues brought to you door, giving you more time to do other things. It also teaches your team self-reliance, problem solving, and self-management.

Touch Rule #3: <u>"Touch" your pipeline every day</u>. Whether you keep your pipeline as a spreadsheet, in your CRM, or by some other method, make it the first thing you look at in the morning, and the last thing you look at before you go home. Look at it several times in between. Ask yourself, and your reps, "What can we do to move each deal just one step forward?" This simple exercise will help you dictate your priorities, the priorities of your reps, and help you achieve your real purpose, therefore helping everyone on your team to do better and achieve results.

Stand and Give Recognition

7 Truths and 7 Best Practices for Recognizing Sales People

As we discussed in the chapter "The Mind of the Sales Rep," all sales people live and die by three basic motivational factors. Those are **money, freedom, and recognition.** Many experienced managers believe that recognition is, by far, the most important of the three. Recognition takes some work on your part as a sales manager, but many sales managers find it to be the most fun and rewarding part of the job.

Recognition is critical in all departments, but it is simply irreplaceable on a sales team. Here are **seven simple truths and seven best practices** about recognition:-

Truth #1 – If you don't recognize your sales people, someone else will, and they will leave.

Truth #2 – Sales people are hard-wired for recognition. They literally need recognition to be content.

Truth #3 – Recognition can, and should, come in many forms, from the expensive to the free.

Truth #4 – Recognition is not motivation. You actually cannot motivate anyone. People motivate themselves. You must create an environment that allows them to become motivated by their own desires.

Truth #5 – Recognition must be GENUINE. You must mean it and show that you mean it. It cannot be connected to an agenda or ulterior motive.

Truth #6 – Recognition must be PERSONAL and SPECIFIC. If you give out a trophy, it must have the reps name, the date, and the specifics of the award. i.e.

Ed Cowdrey

September Sales Rep of the Month

111% of Quota.

When the time comes for you to hand out the award, cite specifics of the sales rep's accomplishments. There is a big difference between "great work" and "Ed was able achieve this milestone by bringing in three deals worth more than $100k in revenue", "His customers rave about his attention to detail". One customer said this: "We bought from Ed because he took the time to understand our business and develop a custom solution for our specific needs".

Truth #7 – Recognition must be PUBLIC and TIMELY. First, don't let too much time go by before you show recognition. It loses meaning and effect if the proximity to the event is too far away. As a rule, no more than 30 days should elapse. Immediate is better. Second, telling someone "good job" in your office is nice, but doesn't get the job done or produce any real effect. Make it public. It must be by email, voice mail, a conference call, or walking them up in front of the room.

The question then becomes...

How you put these truths into practice? Below is a list of "must do" recognition activities. Some of these may be beyond you immediate control as a sales manager, but are considered to be the most important recognition practices for a sales team.

Practice #1 – President's Club (a.k.a. Circle of Excellence, the big trip at the end of the year). While I was at IKON, we did numerous employee satisfaction surveys every year. The NUMBER ONE most motivating form of recognition for the sales team was the President's Club Trip. As a sales manager, it is important to use this event to the maximum motivation possible. How do you maximize the motivation? Publish stack rankings of how each rep is progressing toward the qualifying goal. Do this on a regular basis (monthly). Print them and hang them on your door. Email them. Talk about them during team meetings.

Practice #2 – Sales Rep of the Month Award – I have seen a lot of companies eliminate this for reasons that I cannot begin to fathom. This is a MUST DO. Get the team together either in person or virtually, and recognize the number one performer on the team from the prior month. This is a big deal and should be conducted as such.

Do NOT give out certificates! No one gives two cents about a silly piece of paper. Ever try hanging a piece of paper in a cube? It doesn't work well and is an insult to the award and to the recipient because it is CHEAP and says you really don't care about the award or the achievement. It actually undermines the accomplishment.

GIVE OUT A TROPHY! There are hundreds of on-line trophy stores and you can get custom engraved crystal trophies with your company's logo for less than $50.00. Go find something that fits your team, your company, and make it your theme, **and, don't forget the money!** Every trophy should be accompanied by at least a $25 gift card. More is better. Fight for the budget and give out $100 AMEX gift cards if you can. The impact and desire to win goes through the roof.

One of the most effective recognition programs we ever witnessed was one by a regional manager down in Texas. He handed out giant silver BULL trophies. Yep! Huge silver bull trophies with horns and hooves. It was a large office, but to walk through it and see dozens, perhaps a hundred, 12" tall silver bulls sitting on top of (not in) all the cubes was impressive even for an outsider. It was brilliant! No rep in that office could stand to be without at least one bull. Talk about a motivational environment!

Practice #3 – Stack Rankings – There is NO PRESSURE like PEER PRESSURE. Publicize the monthly stack rankings (performance vs. plan) for your team and show them how they stack up against each other and against other teams. You will not have to say a word. Post them everywhere.

Practice #4 – Customer Feedback – When a customer writes an email or letter describing the good deeds of a rep, show it off! It's FREE and it has great impact on the other members of the team, making them want the same feedback. They will therefore emulate the behavior.

Practice #5 – Ring the Bell – Perhaps the oldest tradition in professional sales. The iconic brass bell that sales reps ring when they bring in a deal. These days, very few offices hang a bell. That is too bad. If you can't hang and use a bell, use email, or send an email to the entire team with RING THE BELL in the subject line. In the body of the email, congratulate the rep and detail the deal they closed. They will love it. They will want to do it again and again. It also builds pressure on the rest of the team.

Practice #6 – Be open to new ideas and do not be repetitive. Sure, you have to award the sales rep of the month award, but do not let yourself get stuck with the same old two awards you hand out every month. Be creative! Give out a "Going Above And Beyond" award to mark something special. Maybe a rep showed up early on a Saturday to support a weekend install? Recognize it! Make it fun! Give out the "Stayed Up All Night To Complete The Bid" award. Make it fun and make it count.

Practice #7 – Be Cross Functional. One of the best practices your team can share is to act as team and give an award to a service tech, or an admin staff, who supports your team. Bring the recipient into a team meeting and give them an award (trophy rule and money rule applies!). You will win undying support for your team and your team will feel good about the "giving" aspect just like you feel good when you give recognition to them.

Road Warrior or Road Worrier?

15 Lessons to Make Life on the Road Just a Little Easier

It is Monday morning, 5:40 AM, and I have just boarded the flight from Richmond to Charlotte. I have already been up for two hours and 29 minutes, so that I could take a shower and get to the airport. As I sit down, I recognize many of the faces. The faces are the same as they are almost every Monday morning. Most people on this flight are business travelers, and this is the start of their week.

The thing about the 5:40 AM flight is that it is always silent. People are silent when they board. People are silent when they sit down. The crew is even silent except for their courteous greetings. Most of the regular travelers know the crew and the crew knows us. No one wants to be up this early, but it is what we do. Then, as the flight is almost loaded and I am almost asleep, it happens…on rushes a young guy, suit and tie on, dragging not one, but three carryon bags. You can see the fresh sheen of sweat on his brow from his rush to the gate. I turn and watch him go by in half amusement and half frustration. His mismatched luggage bumps nearly everyone sitting on the aisle. He cannot find enough overhead storage space, so he ends up jamming his bags into two different overhead bins and one under his feet. He has a window seat, so the two people on the aisle and center, who were somewhat settled in, have to get up and move for him to get in his seat, while he beats his bag against three more people. He finally settles in and then realizes he still has his suit coat on. Now he tries to stand and remove it. He pops the lady next to him in the back of the head with his elbow and the whole plane is watching.

Thank goodness that I am lucky enough to have been upgraded to First Class this morning and do not have to deal with this guy at this hour. Those of us up front share one thing in common…a lot of travel. Regular travel at least means upgrades to First Class and seating with the regular travelers who know how to behave. Being up front means we can get a drink before we leave the ground and be in a comfortable enough seat to actually sleep the 43 minutes it takes to get to Charlotte. I hope those people sitting back there near the amateur are half as lucky to get some sleep.

Besides the extra room, the other reason we can sleep is that we have enough travel experience to not be worried about anything involving the actual trip.

I swear I could get from Richmond to over twenty cities without even thinking about what gate I needed to find. Here are some of the lessons I have learned about business travel. Some I learned the hard way. Some I learned from other seasoned professionals.

Here is the message: as a Sales Manager, it is very likely you will be required to travel. Some more than others, but you will likely travel as part of your duties. Take these lessons to heart and sleep better on the next segment to where ever you are going.

Travel Lesson 1 – Become loyal to an airline. Pick and airline and stick with it. Do not use multiple carriers! I know, many companies have policies about these things. I would never suggest you circumvent the policies, but I would suggest you find every way possible to follow this advice. There are several reasons that benefit both you and the company. Benefits to you include upgrades to first class, boarding first, preferred access lines to go through security, and lots of air miles you can use for yourself. Benefits to your company include getting more work out you when you sit in first class because you actually have the room to work, no baggage fees, reduced change fees, and a happier employee.

Travel Lesson 2 – Become loyal to a hotel chain. This is the same idea as with the airplane program. The rewards programs have gotten pretty good including upgrades to suites, points multipliers, free breakfasts, and much more.

Travel Lesson 3 – Become loyal to a car rental company. Same idea as with airlines and hotels, but this one can really save you time. Many rental car companies have "bypass the counter" programs for loyalty members. This can save you huge amounts of time when are rushing to make that meeting after your flight landed late. The free rental car days you accumulate are also a nice perk.

Travel Lesson 4 – Learn the airports. If you travel allot, you will want to try to frequent certain routes and certain airports. I fly through Charlotte allot because it is a great airport. It is well-managed, clean, and has good food! It rarely has delays, lost baggage, or other problems. Get a feature map of the airports you go to most. Learn the layout, the location of the best eateries, best wine bars, etc. You will get stuck from time to time. Learn to make the most of it and be comfortable with where you are. It will save you time and frustration.

Travel Lesson 5 – Sign up for TSA Pre-Check. Many airport TSA security lines are adding the TSA Pre-Check line. It can be the difference between walking right through security or standing in line for an hour. You can register through your airline if you are a frequent flyer, or you can go online and register. It is well worth it! Once registered, you do not have to take off your shoes, belt, or anything else. You can also leave your laptop in the bag. It makes the process very fast and very convenient.

Travel Lesson 6 – Learn how to book flight connections. Okay, here are my three rules for booking connections.

One, never take the first flight out unless you have to. When you have to get up at 3:00 AM, you are not worth 10 cents in terms of mental acuity by the time lunch rolls around.

Two, never book connections any closer together than 45 minutes. Airlines will actually let you book connections that are just 30 minutes apart. Think about that. The door for the next flight is supposed to close at 10 minutes till the flight. In reality that almost never happens, but it can happen. That leaves you 20 minutes to get off your flight and go to the next gate. If your first flight is just 10 minutes late, you will be literally running through the airport to find the next gate.

Three, never take a red-eye. You will not get any real sleep and you will be ruined for the entire next day.

Travel Lesson 7 – Carry a book. You still cannot use a reader or an iPad while the plane is loaded. The FAA has proposed to change this rule and it may be changed by the time this is published, however, you cannot currently use any electronic device until you get to 10,000 feet (that's when you hear the BING BING sound). So what are you going to do for the 30 minutes while the plane loads, taxis, and comes to altitude? Work? I doubt it, unless you have a bunch of paper with you. Even if you do, you can't put the table down. After a flight or two, you will have read every article of this month's airline magazine! Carry a book. It will pass the time and keep your mind engaged on something healthy. Once the FAA finally changes the rule, you will still want to carry a book. Leaders are readers, the more you read, the more you gain mentally and the more you start thinking outside of the day-to-day grind. Whether you choose paper books, electronic readers, or a book application for tablets, reading is a must for sales managers.

Travel Lesson 8 – Carry an iPad or other tablet. Easy and fast to connect to the internet with start-up time like a PC. Need I say more? How about having your own music and movies with you? Time on flights can be incredibly tedious. This is a must have.

Travel Lesson 9 – Check your bag. I know there are two schools of thought on this, but I do not understand why anyone would want to drag their big bag onto the plane after dragging it all the way through the airport. You have to fight the crowds, fight to get it into the overhead bin, fight to get it down, and many planes don't have the space, so you have to check it at the gate anyway. Why would anyone do this? Just to save a few minutes at your destination while waiting for the carousel to deliver your bag at your final destination? Afraid it's going to get lost? The math just doesn't work.

Here's why you should check your bag. One, the odds of your bag getting lost are really small. In over 400 flights, my bag has only been delayed a few times and never lost. The airlines will tell you that less than .0001% of all bags that get "lost." Two, it makes your travel more relaxing. Try going from gate to gate in Chicago or Atlanta while you drag your suitcase, laptop bag, and whatever else you're carrying. You'll move at a snail's pace and add stress to your trip. Three, you can use a bigger bag like a rolling garment bag. The result is, your clothes don't look like you've slept in them when you arrive. Four, you may actually save time because you don't have to carry a bunch of specialty cosmetics that have to be removed and inspected at every security check point.

Travel Lesson 10 – Never eat at chain restaurants. Once you have a job that requires a lot of travel, you will quickly find that all the glamour of business is a farce. Business travel is a grind. You must find little ways to enjoy the travel or give up and get another job. Chain restaurants are predictably boring and the same everywhere you go. That should be a plus, but in practice, it's not. Take the opportunity to go to restaurants that are not chains. Get out and enjoy the local flavor, custom, and individualism that surround you. Add some fun to travel. I spent most of last year trying to eat at every restaurant from Man vs. Food when I was in the town that the show had been to. The food was awesome and it was a hell of a lot more from fun than eating at Friday's!

Travel Lesson 11 – Get yourself a decent suitcase (or set) – It never ceases to amaze me when I fly to a city, go to a meeting and then look at the people who appear to have slept in their suit. Get yourself a good bag or set of bags. It will help you keep your belongings nicer, newer, and you will look more professional.

Travel Lesson 12 – Get yourself some really comfortable shoes – Most dress shoes, even expensive ones, are not made for a great deal for walking. If you travel a lot, you will be walking a lot. Once, I sat next to a guy on an airplane once who was wearing a pair of leather "driver" shoes. They looked professional, yet very comfortable. He told me he wore them whenever he flew. I now own two pairs and it was the best self-investment I made in years.

Travel Lesson 13 – Get yourself a set of good baggage tags – The details matter and this is a detail that is overlooked. You never know when you will have to check a bag with an airline, or leave it in a hotel, or check it at meeting site. Good tags help protect your belongings and make it easier for your bag to be recognized.

Travel Lesson 14 – Treat the airline and hotel staff with complete courtesy – It amazes me how many times I have watched some traveler yelling and screaming at gate agents or hotel clerks about problems with reservations, cancelled flights and a whole host of other problems. This is nothing short of stupid. The old saying about gathering flies with honey really, really works. No gate agent is responsible for your delayed flight, so why take it out on them. They cannot control the situation any more than you can. If you travel, there will be problems. Learn to accept that as a fact. Learn to relax, be nice, and look at every problem as chance to get some extra work done, try some wine you haven't had before, or read. Make something positive out of it or you will drive yourself crazy. Plus, go yell at a gate agent or a hotel clerk and see how much help you actually get.

Travel Lesson 15 – Come in the night before the meeting. Given the choice between getting up really early and coming in the night before, choose the night before every time. You will be better prepared, more engaged, more productive, and have less stress because you will not be worrying about flight delays and other travel related stressors.

Managing Superman – the Prima-Donna Rep

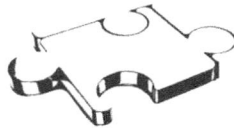

6 Rules to Dealing with the Prima-Donna on Your Team

We all know at least one *"Superman."* That one sales rep who is convinced they are the world's gift to sales. They are quite sure that the rules, expectations, and standards for everyone else do not apply to them. And why should the rules apply? After all, "Superman" hits his/her numbers every month, every quarter, and every year. They hold all the sales records. Just look at the score board! "Superman" doesn't need to attend meetings, training, attend conference calls, fill out reports, use the company CRM, or even maintain a calendar. Just look at the scoreboard! "Superman" expects to be privileged. "Superman" expects that the company will bend to his/her will because, well, just look at the scoreboard!

Let's face it. Great sales people are really hard to find. Once we find them, we want to keep them. As a sales manager, at some point in your career, you will have at least one "Superman" on your team and you may consider them to be a blessing and a curse. How do we as sales managers harness the high energy 'good' of "Superman" and minimize the negative? How do we manage the high-flying, type ultra A, swaggering into the meeting, "Superman?"

Before we get to the "how," let me tell you a story about my "Superman." (This goes back a few years, and I have changed the names to protect the guilty.) Let's call him Dario. Dario had been with the company for 15 years. He had also made President's Club for 12 out of those 15 years. He almost always made his number. Dario could be counted on to make his forecast an amazing 90% of the time. He was well-respected as a product expert and most customers seemed to have genuine trusting relationships with him. Dario regularly won contests, made lots of money, and was usually ranked among the top 10% of his peers on every stack ranking report that came out. Dario was a self-proclaimed "sales stud." All you had to do was ask him.

Managing Dario was another story. He had seen sales managers come and go and was convinced he could outlast me and anyone else who came along. He was regularly late to meetings. Once in team meetings, he would not pay attention, would argue with guests to the meeting, surf the web, be negative about anything and everything, and criticize anything that represented change. Dario was always late coming into the office and the first to leave. He would park himself in my office every Monday and tell me how the company was all screwed up, how he was getting screwed by the company, how every system and process was broken, and why we needed more territory and a smaller budget. He would literally tell me, "Just look at the scoreboard; the guy at the top should get treated better." He would refuse to use the company CRM and would not keep his calendar up to date. He would refuse any and all forms of accountability.

Dario was also a test of any manager in terms of pushing behavioral limits. Once, when on a team training trip, he managed to get himself arrested and spent the night in jail. Somehow, the company decided to keep him. Next, on another company trip to a meeting, he had a few too many cocktails and decided to proposition one of the young female reps, who had recently joined the company. Even that was not enough to end his career, although it would have been the career ender for almost anyone else. Of course, this served to only bolster his opinion of his own self-worth.

At this point, it was either going to be Dario or me. After a "sit down" with my manager and HR, we all agreed, together, that we would explain to Dario that he had used up all of his "nine lives." When that meeting finally happened, I made sure it was me doing the talking, as a symbolic message of who his manager was and who was going to be helping him or not, as the case may be. Dario and I finally got our relationship ironed out, and we got his behavior under control for the most part. It took a lot of work, effort, and commitment.

Most "Superman" reps are not as extreme as Dario. Most are shades of someone far less challenging. Below are some suggestions for dealing with your superman.

Superman Rule 1: Look in the mirror – As a sales manager, you need to make a critical decision. Am I willing

to coach this employee differently than others? Am I willing
to invest the extra time and attention required? Am I willing
to play the game in order to maximize performance? You
must make a conscious decision. If you answer YES, then
the rest of the rules will help you. If you answer NO, then be
prepared to hold the line and 'let the chips fall where they
may'.

Superman Rule 2: Get your manager's support – It
is critical that you have a behind closed doors discussion
with your manager about your "Superman" and discuss
options, strategies, tactics, and potential outcomes. Other
managers and employees who are as little as one step
removed from your team, will likely see and perceive your
"Superman" differently than you do. Getting your manager's
support will serve to inform them of the situation, protect
you, and help you find answers to some of the most
important questions regarding your overall strategy in
managing "Superman." Perhaps the most important thing is
to establish and gain agreement with your manager about the
decision that "Superman" will NOT be allowed a different
set of rules than the other reps on your team. *Allowing
"Superman" to live by a different set of rules will undermine
your authority and the morale of the entire team.*

Superman Rule 3: Play into the ego – Your
"Superman" will, most likely, have a gigantic ego. Use that
to your advantage. Pull him/her into your office and lavish
with praise before you start asking for changes to their
behavior. Explain how "as the most valuable player" on the
team, they have the opportunity to be a leader in multiple
ways, including not just results, but attitude, gratitude and
company messaging. Explain to them why these "additions"

are good for them and their career. Explain that visibility is their best asset and they should be looking to invest in that asset, letting it be an anchor for how they are perceived by others. Trust me, they care about how people see them. *If you order the discussion points as praise/constructive criticism/praise, "Superman" will usually react well and leave feeling good about the message.*

Superman Rule 4: Set the Same Expectations in a Different Way – Superman will most likely pay little or no regard to the expectations you set for the team. When this happens, you will need to find different ways to gain their buy in. One of the great managers we know likes to go through each of the team expectations, one by one, and let their "Superman" tell them everything that is wrong with the expectation and why it doesn't apply. Often, allowing superman to vent is all that is required.

One of the best lessons I have learned to teach is the 'praise in public, complain in private rule'. When you sit "Superman" down alone in your office and ask, beg and plead with them to get on board, you must let them know that this is the ONE single rule they must follow. You CANNOT and WILL NOT allow them to be the rotten apple in the bushel. They simply cannot buck you or your message in front of others.

What really works is this: focus them on THEIR goals. Of course, you must understand what their goals really are. You must take the time and energy to understand what is genuinely important to them. Once you know that, you can build every expectation around why it helps them to achieve their goals. Have them list their goals and relate it to each expectation. They may get frustrated at first, but this really works.

Superman Rule 5: Teach them differently – "Superman" may not be someone who can sit through a training class without feeling the need to demonstrate their expertise to everyone in the room. One proven method that forces people to learn, is giving them the role of teacher. Assigning "Superman" a presentation to the rest of the team does two things to improve the issue. One, it forces them to learn, sometimes things they were not willing to admit they did not know. Two, it feeds their ego and makes them feel important as an expert.

Another great method… Give them something extra to do which they will perceive as important. Perhaps that means mentoring a younger rep. Perhaps that means assigning them to some special project. Perhaps that means getting them assigned to some special advisory council.

Superman Rule 6: Rinse and Repeat – Be prepared to invest time in "Superman." You may need to reiterate the expectations, the rules, and reinstall the idea of conformity on a regular basis. As always, inspect what you expect, and be prepared to send frequent "reminders" of tasks or behaviors that need to be completed.

A final note: Most "Superman" reps are great people who mean well for themselves and the company. They are worth keeping. They just need to be made to feel special. You may just simply need to explain in clear terms that certain behaviors are simply conditions of employment … period.

As managers, we occasionally have to make the hard choice that regardless of performance, they are not worth keeping. They are simply too abrasive or too disruptive to the organization and have to go. Always be prepared to have the managerial courage to do the right thing, regardless of the revenue that may be associated with it. In the case above, Dario should have been terminated long before he left the company, but reality is often harder than it appears. The balance lies in whether "Superman" is ultimately lifting the team up or dragging them down.

13 Principals of Sales Management Ethics

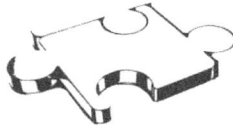

Liar, Liar, Profits on Fire!

FACT: **Companies deemed ethical outperform unethical companies by 370%** (*According to an index study by Journal of Business and Economics and published by prnewswire.com*).

Ethical companies attract new customers, keep their employees, keep their existing customers, and can exercise value pricing higher than the market (see the same study).

In light of this, the unfortunate truth is we see and hear about poor and sometimes intentional, unethical behavior far too often. We see it on Facebook, LinkedIn, the news, email, etc. Yet, there seems to be an overwhelming tide of cheats, liars, and flat-out fraud being committed in the business world. The good news is that the world has a funny way of catching up to cheats and liars. It is rare for any company to have been created and to grow and prosper based on a weak or unethical foundation. Almost always, things come back to bite them and take them down. So why do people fail to act ethically? That is perhaps another story, but it seems there are too many people and companies focused upon "getting rich quick" instead of getting rich <u>right</u>.

Getting fired, having a bad reputation, losing deals, losing customers, losing valued employees, and possibly going to jail are the things that can happen without good ethics. In today's world of the internet, of customer peer groups, social media, and instant communication, you cannot run and you cannot hide from bad behavior. The other side of that particular coin, acting honorably, with good ethical standards, can be highly rewarding, highly profitable, bring recognition, earn more business, and be much less stressful.

Anyone who has spent any time at all in a business environment has likely seen the practice of good ethical behavior and of course, the opposite. We usually know what good looks like when we see it. Putting good ethics into practice can sometimes be difficult especially if we have had "teachers" who did not always show us the right way, or if we have been in environments that encouraged something less.

As a manager, you will be faced with decisions every day. Some of these decisions will be small; some will be very large and impactful. Below are some ethical practices to consider.

Set the Bar High – <u>At least</u> once or twice a year; cover your company's ethics policy with your team. Let them know this is a serious matter and infractions will not be tolerated. Let them know this the baseline of the company's mission.

Earn and Create Trust – Create an environment of trust. Trust must happen between employees and between the company and customers. Customers want and need to trust you, your team, and your company. When customers stop trusting you, they leave. You must demonstrate trust. The best way to do that is to be honest. If you, or someone on your team makes a mistake, own up to it and do what you can to fix it. Trust is also earned by doing what you say you will do. If you make a commitment, stick to it. That doesn't mean you can do half of the promise either. Do what you say and people will trust you. Insist you team follows this rule. When employees do not trust leadership it handcuffs the entire operation and profits suffer.

Bad News Does Not Get Better With Time – When you are faced with delivering some news, information, any message that you feel may be perceived as negative, it is better to do it as quickly as possible. That is not to say you should rush, rather, you should prepare, structure, and deliver the message as soon as is reasonably possible. Most of the time, you have learned about the negative news well before your team. Once you tell them, be prepared to let them vent and let them process the information. They will get through it and move on just like you did.

No Spin Zone – Most of us have known managers who tried to spin or soften certain negative messages. Don't do it. Your team is smart. They are probably smarter than you give them credit for. They will see through the spin. Give them the truth. Show them the many sides of the story, but always give them the truth. Employees will appreciate your honesty and may even come to you with solutions you had not considered.

A Doctrine of Fairness – Sales reps tend to make decisions according to a simple ranking system:- Rep first, customer next, company last. Owners and managers tend to reverse the ranking:- Company first, customer second, rep last. Often the answer lies in finding answers that are good for all involved. If the answer isn't good for everyone, then the answer probably isn't the best one.

Never, Never, NEVER Lie – As a manager, there will be things you know are not allowed to disclose. If someone on your team asks you about such a subject, it is better to say "I know, but I cannot discuss it. I will be happy to address it with you as soon as I am able. I hope you can understand." Guess what? They will understand and they will appreciate your honesty. Managers who lie aren't trusted and they encourage their employees to copy their behavior.

Turn On the Light – Transparency of information is key to the health, culture, and good ethics of your team. Share as much as you can with them as often as you can. Maybe cover "new" information on your weekly team calls or some other regular schedule. Cover anything and everything you can. Go through the company financials, even if they are not great. Go through new initiatives. Go through developments from other parts of the company.

Your team will appreciate the fact that you are not "hiding" information from them. Let's face it – there are very few secrets in most companies. This is especially true in small companies when the actions of the owner or senior manager are one thing and their words are another. Most of the time there is a reasonable explanation for these contradictions, but failure to address such matters will lead to employees drawing a negative conclusion.

Rumor Control – The amount and frequency of rumors varies from company to company. Most big companies are like big ships, they have a lot of leaks. Take time with your team to air out all the recent rumors and address them one at a time. Failure to do this can make it appear as though you are hiding information or avoiding a difficult subject. This can be viewed as condoning or supporting bad behavior. Failure to do so can even go so far as to undermine the morale and the corporate mission.

The Comp Plan is Not a Weapon – Comp and ethics are woven together like fabric. A sales rep lives, dies, eats, and breathes by the comp plan. Do not let anyone use it as "technicality" in order to delay or avoid payment to your rep. Vague and ambiguous comp plans are the company's issue, not the rep's. As a manager you need to fight for your rep and insist on a better written comp plan vs. not paying a rep after the sale. Business owners and senior managers need to be aware that this is a serious ethical breach and these employees will leave the company. Make them aware and encourage everyone to do the right thing. The sword cuts both ways. Let your reps know that claiming commissions they plainly have not earned is an ethics violation.

Stomp Out Unethical Behavior Quickly and Severely – Once you become aware that an employee is engaged in lying, cheating, stealing, writing side letters, making false promises to customers, or anything else that may violate the company's ethics policy, put an immediate stop to it. That means correcting the behavior and terminating the employee, even if they are your top performer. Other employees will get the message and any behavior you are not aware of will likely stop. Be prepared to be honest with customers and make amends when a customer situation is involved. Doing so can save the customer relationship. Failure to do so can, and will, cost the company profits and even open the company up too serious liability.

Manage Up – This can very difficult, but it needs to happen. Sometimes a middle manager, maybe your manager, might be perceived by the front line employees as being unethical or being engaged in some questionable behavior. Address it! Depending on your company culture, there are lots of ways to do this. You can go to them directly. You can go to one of their peers. You can go to their boss (do this last). Most of the time, the middle manager does not recognize the perception of the others and will appreciate your raising the issues, as long as you do it in a caring and professional way.

Be Prepared to Run – If you find yourself working for a company that is engaged in unethical behavior, you may need to leave, especially if you do not feel you can change it. When that happens, get out as fast as you can. There are companies out there that are just plain poorly run with really bad leaders. Don't associate yourself with them.

Eventually, the truth always comes out and they will have problems. You do not want customers and other people in your industry to associate you with unethical behavior.

Reward the Good – When you find a situation where an employee was faced a difficult choice and they did the right thing – reward them! Reward them big and publicly. This takes you full circle back to the policy and encouraging all your employees to do the right thing.

Teach Them to Fish

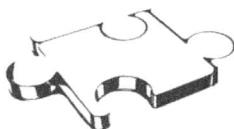

6 Lessons for Training Your Sales Team

Someone once said that "training is a journey, not a destination", and it is the truth. To your sales team, training is pure gold. It is so valuable that it can be directly correlated to success at almost every level and measured in every key performance indicator. One of my all time favorite sales leaders used to explain the importance of training using "the lumberjack theory." That is, "if you do not stop and sharpen your axe every now and then, cutting down the trees gets harder and harder."

As a sales manager, one of your primary tasks is coaching everyone on your team to perform at a higher level. The most significant coaching activity you can perform is regular training for your team. That doesn't mean you have to do all the training. Rather, you must ensure your team is getting trained. Most companies have invested in a variety of training programs, but it is important you don't stop there. There are several keys to good sales training. Consider all of these when planning your team's learning.

Learning is not a one way street. Remember that people learn in different ways. There are three types of primary learning; reading, watching, and doing. Most people are a combination of all three, but we all have a dominant preferred method. Good coaching on your part means exposing your team to all three methods.

How do you eat an elephant? One bite at a time. Training for sales people needs to be a regular event, not just a two day trip. Many companies make the mistake of believing that if we send the sales teams off to train for a week, they will finish the training and be ready to run. The truth is that rarely works with sales people. Most sales people cannot sit still for more than an hour, much less several days. The best sales training is given in regular, short, intense bursts. One to three 50 minute sessions per week will yield better results and your reps will appreciate the regularity and structure. They will absorb more information. They will be able to go and apply what they have learned immediately.

According to The American Society for Training and Development, one week after sales training, the average salesperson will lose up to 70% of the new skills they learned but did not use. The point is not that off site, multi-day training programs are all bad. They do serve some good purposes such as team building, exposure to the company, and focused learning. That said, you cannot allow it to take the place of a more regular schedule. Rather, it is a supplement or a booster to your team's normal training program. If you have the chance to take your team to see their product being manufactured, or to the office where orders are processed, or to a service center, or a customer's site, you should absolutely take advantage of these irreplaceable experiences for your team members, but it cannot serve as their only training.

Rules during training sessions. Once you get everyone together for a training session, it is critical you set some hard-line expectations and rules so that everyone gets the most out of the session. You cannot allow anyone to violate the rules. If you allow exceptions, the sessions will quickly fall apart. The following are an example of rules to set.

1) Everyone on the team attends all sessions. No exceptions. No calling in saying "The customer can only see me at this time."

2) No cell phones, laptops, iPads, or other electronic distractions. They must turn them off or leave them at their desks. The first time a cell phone rings, take it and return it when the meeting is over.

3) No leaving the meeting. Let them know, this is a 50 minute session and they should go to the bathroom prior to starting.

4) Start on time and end on time. Your team will appreciate the structure and work their calendar around the training once they believe you are serious and will respect their time.

5) Respect for everyone. Everyone needs to remember that team members may be at different levels of expertise in regards to various subject matters. Team members must be respectful of each other's struggles and helpful whenever possible.

Train your team on everything. The list of subject matter is important. It should be mixed, so a variety of skill sets overlap. Sticking to one subject for too long can be boring and lose its effectiveness. Here are some of the most important skill sets to bring to your team:

1) Product training – Sales people are expected to be the subject matter experts on what they sell. Regular and detailed product training and testing is a requirement.

2) Process training – Often overlooked, but critical to the sales role. Train your team on everything from site surveys, to getting an order through the system, to your service process.

3) Prospecting – How many ways can a sales rep prospect? Teach them cold calling (good old door knocking), the telephone, email, professional networking groups, LinkedIn and other social media, the written letter (a lost art, but very effective), and all the other methods your company finds productive. The key is teaching them to do ALL of them, not just the one or two they are comfortable with.

4) Closing Skills – How many closes does each member of your team know? How many do they use? Most Business to Business deals require that the rep hears the

word "No" 3 to 8 times before a deal gets closed. Teach them how to ask for the order in several different ways.

5) Presentation Skills – Sales people are often hired for their presentation skills. Good now, but does now mean good in a year? This skill set is constantly evolving with technology. Make sure your team knows how to deliver something other than a PowerPoint slide deck as a presentation. Make sure they know how to utilize multimedia, effective speaking, questioning, customer engagement, and other modern presentation skills.

6) Demonstration skills – What more critical skill set can a sales rep have? Drill, drill, drill your company's product demonstration on a regular basis. Have the best of your team show off their skills. Have your team share real world demo wins, tips, tricks, pitfalls, objections, and other experiences.

7) Resource Usage – Does your team know how to navigate the various resources and support systems within your company? Teach them how. It will save you time. It will save them time.

8) Competitor Training – Does your team know your competition as well as they know their own product? Can they have an intelligent discussion with a customer about a competitor without bashing the competition?

9) Industry Training – What are the latest developments and trends in your industry? Who are the news makers and why?

10) Objection handling – What are the top 10 objections your team hears from customers? How do they overcome these objections? This is a great opportunity to round-table each objection and then listen to how each rep handles the situation.

Death by PowerPoint. We know. It is almost impossible to get away from. How many endless meetings and training sessions have you been to where you sat in your seat all day and viewed 100 slides? Your sales team should be pleasantly surprised when they show up for training. The sessions should feature different approaches. Here are some ideas to keep the training sessions fresh, fun, and interactive.

1) No PowerPoint. Use a white board or flip chart and write out ideas as you discuss them. The reps will stay engaged and learn more.

2) Bring in different presenters. Bring in trainers, other managers, customers, highly successful reps, vendors, industry experts, and even have members of your team present. It doesn't always have to be you or the corporate trainer presenting. Let the guest presenter know that PowerPoint is either not allowed, or only allowed to display pictures, not words.

3) Make them read a book. There are so many great sales books out there, yet too many sales people do not make a study of their own profession. Make them read a book and discuss it as a training session.

4) Take the chairs out of the training room (unless physically necessary for anyone). Have everyone stand

around the product as you teach. This will keep them engaged and force them to put their hands on the sessions.

5) Gamification. Gamification is defined as "The use of game thinking and game mechanics in non-game contexts to engage users in solving problems" (Wikipedia). There is much being written about this subject lately. Do some research and try it out. You will need to find exercises that are relevant to your industry.

6) Change of Venue. Change the location of the training sessions. Do some over the web, some in the conference room, some off site, some at a customer's site, and some at a related facility such as a manufacturing center if possible.

Remote Training. If your sales team is spread out and cannot get together on a regular basis, there are still a number of methods you can use to keep the training fresh, interactive and inspiring. These are complimentary to the list above.

1) When you on-board a new remote sales rep, bring them to HQ for a week or two. This will excite them about their decision to come to work with you, allow them to put names to the faces of their support structure and be in an environment where they can focus on learning. Have their tools ready to go. Have their laptop, phone, demo kit and other tools personalized, complete and fully functional when they arrive. This way they can focus on learning and not setting up. Never, never put the "burden of training" on the sales rep. Good sales people by nature tend to be Type A, easily distracted, and focused on only the things they deem

important. That's good. It's why you hired them. Take advantage of their strengths and give them a road to follow. Too many companies put out these "self-paced" training programs. That may work for administrative staff, but sales people either will not do it or will put in the minimum effort required. Have an interactive training program and agenda they can follow with tight deadlines. You will need to check in with them regularly (at least daily) to make sure they are on track.

2) Use video calls for remote sales teams. There are dozens of video meeting solutions. Some are free or very cheap. This will ensure everyone stays engaged and doesn't get distracted.

3) Use electronic white boards instead of PowerPoint whenever possible. Most of these come with the video call solutions.

4) Call out members of the team for questions and opinions. Again, this keeps everyone on their toes and engaged, instead of checking stock prices.

5) Use multimedia such as video clips, or flash presentations. Visual imaging is very powerful and your team will retain more information.

Are you a Leader or a Bleeder?

38 Principals of Leadership for Sales Managers

Are you leading your team to success, or bleeding them for results?

Much and more has been written about leadership. As a sales manager, you need to decide what kind of leader you want to be. Most of us tend to try and emulate the good leaders we have worked with, while turning away from our personal experiences of styles we did not like. Deciding what kind of leader you want to be can make or break your career.

The study of "leadership" could likely lead to a Ph.D. with the amount of information available. Just Google "Types of leadership" and you will find there are two types, three types, four types, eight types, ten types, etc. It is important you take time to study leadership and this book is a practical place to start.

To drive a sales team, you must balance driving your team to get the maximum results possible and being a "good" person. Notice that we said "balance." You must be careful to do both. This is backed up by actual data. According to a study (Zenger/Folkman published in the Harvard Business Review), the best leaders are a balance of both: "drivers" and "enhancers." "Drivers" demand excellence, while "enhancers" are more of a role model, treating employees like actual people.

You have likely worked for managers who were "bad" and those who were "good." These labels are a little subjective and as sales people, we are about getting results, so let's be more specific.

The best leaders are great coaches who are willing to serve their people. The worst leaders bleed their teams of everything positive, usually in order to achieve some short-term success. Let's call them "bleeders."

What kind of sales manager makes a "bleeder"?

A "bleeder"...

1) Does not trust his/her people and micro-manages their time. Are they in the office at 8:00 AM sharp? Do they stay until 5:00 PM? A bleeder does not like people to work from home. In short, he/she does not trust the team and fails to treat them as human beings, with lives outside of work.

2) Spends most of his/her time telling the team what they aren't doing rather than focusing on recognition for what they have done.

3) Is a "keyboard commando" and fails to get out in the field to support his/her sales people and engage with customers

4) Is critical of mistakes or poor performance in public

5) Fails to provide frequent and sincere recognition

6) Keeps the team in the dark about company performance, goals, successes, and failures

7) Drives wedges between members of the team politically and socially

8) Uses the comp plan as a weapon to limit a sales reps commission on every technicality and loop-hole

9) Creates a negative team or company culture

10) Fails to address customer issues quickly and sincerely

11) Expects the team to train themselves

12) Fails to coach first and help the team members to learn from mistakes

13) Makes it all about themselves

14) Acts without getting all sides of the story

What kind of sales manager makes a "leader"?

A "leader"...

1) Has genuine compassion and cares about the team

2) Is willing to fight for his/her people

3) Understands that the team who shares best practices, will win more deals

4) Knows the goals of the team members

5) Knows that if he/she helps everyone on the team achieve their goals, then the manager will achieve his/her goals

6) Studies the art of sales management

7) Gives genuine and sincere recognition on a regular basis

8) Is honest, ethical, and treats the team with consistency

9) Understands the team culture is his/her responsibility first

10) Can be both tough and nice at the same time

11) Creates an environment in which the team motivates themselves

12) Coaches every day and supports his/her people

13) Is out in the field with the team on a regular basis

14) Looks to find solutions to problems that are good for the company, the customer, and the team

16) Has the managerial courage to remove the "C" players from the team, after they have had an adequate opportunity to improve

17) Understands that hiring the best people for the team is his/her number one job function

18) Makes sure his/her people get the credit for the team's success

Your title does not give you power, authority, or the ability to lead. Only your actions do. Being a sales leader is really hard. It means striking a balance between achieving what is good for the company, your rep, the customer, your manager, and getting results that exceed expectations.

Great leaders have teams who want to work for them AND get results. That is the leadership measuring stick that counts the most.

Resources for the Sales Manager

Leaders are readers. As a Sales Manager, it is incumbent upon you to study your profession and improve your skill sets. This book is big step in the right direction, so congratulations to you! Below is a recommended reading and resource list. It is by no means complete, but is literature that may offer you some guidance about subjects and skills you find you want to develop.

Good luck to you in your career – and remember, the most important lesson in the book – **build the best team you can and everything else will follow!**

Recommended for you to read

Parker, Sam & Anderson, Mac. *212° The Extra Degree.* Aurora: Simple Truths, 2006. Print.

Anderson, Mac. *212° Service.* Naperville: Simple Truths, 2011. Print.

Anderson, Mac. *Leadership Quotes.* Naperville: Simple Truths, 2011. Print.

Johnson, Spencer, M.D. *Who Moved My Cheese?.* New York: G.P. Putnam's Sons, 1998. Print

Lencioni, Patrick. *The Five Dysfunctions of a Team: A Leadership Fable.* San Francisco: Jossey-Bass, 2002. Print.

Wagner, Rodd & Harter, James, K. Ph.d. *12 The Elements of Great Managing.* New York: Gallup Press, 2006. Print.

Buckingham, Marcus & Coffman, Curt. *First, Break All the Rules.* New York: Simon & Schuster, 1999. Print.

Fox, Jeffrey, J. *How to Become CEO.* New York: Hyperion, 1998. Print.

Tzu, Sun. *The Art of War.* USA: Sweet Water Press, 2006. Print

For your team to read

Gitomer, Jeffrey. *Little Red Book of Selling*. Austin: Bard Press, 2005. Print.

Davis, Kevin. *Getting Into Your Customer's Head.* New York: Times Books, a division of Random House, Inc., 1996. Print.

Johnson, Spencer, M.D. *Who Moved My Cheese?*. New York: G.P. Putnam's Sons, 1998. Print.

Rackham, Neil. *Spin Selling*. New York: McGraw-Hill, Inc., 1988. Print.

Fox, Jeffrey, J. *Secrets of Great Rainmakers*. New York: Hyperion, 2006. Print

About The Author

Ed Cowdrey

Ed started his sales career in retail during college. He took his first business to business sales job selling fax machines for 100% commission. His career developed over a 20+ year period of exceeding sales expectations coupled with a successful track record of leading others to do the same. He has held a variety of positions including first line sales manager roles to regional manager roles to national sales leadership roles including being a partner/owner.

Ed has enjoyed the privilege of working for and learning from world-class organizations, including IKON, Ricoh, Kodak, and Xerox. Over his career he developed cross-functional depth and experience managing multiple teams responsible for Sales, Marketing, Customer Service, Operations, and Services. He has had extensive experience leading, selling, and delivering product solutions across multiple industries, while growing revenues and profits year after year.

He has enjoyed repeated success in sales management by developing organizational agility, developing relationships, building positive team cultures, and launching new programs including an entire new verticalized national sales group while at Ricoh.

Ed, and his wife Pamela enjoy living in rural Virginia where they successfully started a boutique vineyard dedicated to growing high quality Cabernet Sauvignon in Virginia. They have been blessed with three amazing children (Cassandra, Roshelle, and Quin).

Ed considers this book a way to give back and say "thank you" to all the many wonderful people who have helped him throughout his career. It is his wish that others will be able to learn from this text and enjoy some measure of increased success as a result.

Inside The Sales Manager's Guide to Sanity

17 Topics that are highly relevant to the day to day job of being a sales manager. Topics include driving results, motivating your team, interviewing techniques, coaching in the field, managing different types of reps, sales ethics, building accountability, building team identity and culture, leadership practices, recognition ideas, dealing with company politics, and much more!

Real life examples from someone who has "walked the walk" including many humorous side stories.

Over 100 very specific tips, best practices, do's and don'ts, and real life guidelines that will help improve the performance of any sales team.

Notes:

To visit

The Sales Manager's Guide to Sanity
Blog page, simply copy this link or scan this
QR code…

http://edcowdrey.wordpress.com/

To visit

The Sales Manager's Guide to Sanity
Website, simply copy this link or scan this
QR code…

http://www.salesmanagersguidetosanity.com/